Bygone Arran

by Bernard Byrom

On 24th July 1947 King George VI and Queen Elizabeth, accompanied by Princesses Elizabeth and Margaret and also Naval Lieutenant Philip Mountbatten, arrived at Brodick by launch from the cruiser *HMS Superb*. The King was wearing his uniform of Admiral of the Fleet. They were guests of the Duke and Duchess of Montrose for lunch at Brodick Castle, then they went on a five hour tour of the island. A fortnight earlier Princess Elizabeth and Lieutenant Mountbatten had announced their engagement and when the party landed at the pier a group of women standing on top of the waiting room began singing "All the nice girls love a sailor". Between the pier and the castle Elizabeth and Philip occupied the seats behind the chauffeur but after lunch at the castle they drove together in the second car. At the end of the tour of the island the party left from Lochranza aboard *HMS Superb* to join the Royal Train on the mainland to take them back to London.

Text © Bernard Byrom, 2020.
First published in the United Kingdom, 2020,
by Stenlake Publishing Ltd.,
54-58 Mill Square,
Catrine, Ayrshire,
KA5 6RD

Telephone: 01290 551122
www.stenlake.co.uk

ISBN 9781840339000

**The publishers regret that they cannot supply
copies of any pictures featured in this book.**

The books, newspapers and websites listed below were the principal ones used by the author during his research.

Andrew Boyle, *Pictorial History of Arran,* 1994
Undiscovered Scotland *undiscoveredscotland.co.uk*
Arran HideAways *arran-hideaways.co.uk*
Lamlash website *lamasharran.co.uk*
Strathclyde Postcard Club 2020 Newsletters
The Scotsman
Ardrossan & Saltcoats Herald

Introduction

The Isle of Arran, the largest island in the Firth of Clyde, covers an area of 167 square miles and is 56 miles in circumference by road although the Arran Coastal Way is 67 miles long. The extreme length from north to south is 26 miles and its average breadth is 10 miles. The influence of the Atlantic Ocean and the Gulf Stream create a mid-oceanic climate. Among its many attractions are seven golf courses and two whisky distilleries.

Arran was originally part of the kingdom of Dalraida through the Bronze and Iron Ages with Gaelic-speaking inhabitants being ruled from Ireland. Christianity arrived in the 6th century with the founding of a monastery by St Brendan at Kilpatrick. Over the centuries Arran passed through the hands of the Vikings, the Celts, the English, and the Stewart and MacDonald clans. It was also the seat of the Dukes of Hamilton. The imposed evictions of the Clearances in the 1800s, although less severe on Arran than in many parts of Scotland, nevertheless meant that many islanders set sail to North America in search of a better life.

Imposition of stringent taxes after the Union of the Crowns in 1707 led to widespread smuggling of contraband goods and the distillation of illicit whisky for almost 150 years in the 18th and 19th centuries. In 1797 it was estimated that there were about 50 illicit stills producing 'Arran Water', most of it transported off the island to the mainland. In 1829 the island got its first regular steamer service when the Castle Company provided sailings from Glasgow to Brodick and Lamlash every Tuesday and Saturday, returning on Wednesdays and Mondays. In 1834 the company was able to take advantage of the newly-built passenger railway line between Troon and Kilmarnock by advertising a daily steamer service from Troon and Ardrossan to Brodick and Lamlash, complete with rail connections to and from Kilmarnock. In the days of sail Saltcoats was Ayrshire's main port of departure for Arran, but with the advent of the steamers it was superseded by Ardrossan where the steamers connected with horse-drawn stage coaches from Glasgow and Kilmarnock. A railway line was completed from Glasgow to Ardrossan in 1840 and from then on the Glasgow and South Western Railway Company ran trains to connect with the steamers at Ardrossan and the port secured almost all of the Arran trade. The Campbeltown and Glasgow Steam Packet Company also operated a daily service from 1848 to 1970 which called at Lochranza and Pirnmill en route to Campbeltown.

The greatest handicap to the growth of tourism on Arran was the lack of piers. At every village where steamers called, passengers disembarking had to be transferred in small boats and rowed ashore. Eventually piers were built at Brodick in 1872, Lamlash in 1884, Lochranza in 1889 and finally Whiting Bay in 1901. Until the 1930s steamers still called regularly at Corrie, King's Cross and Pirnmill and occasionally at Machrie, Blackwaterfoot and Kildonan, even though no pier was ever built at these places. In 1890 the Glasgow & South Western Railway came into competition with the Caledonian Railway who had opened a new line from Glasgow to Ardrossan and built a new ship, *Duchess of Hamilton*. The Glasgow & South Western Railway retaliated by introducing the *Glen Sannox*. Competition between the two railway companies and their employees was intense and the late David L Smith tells in his book *Tales of the Glasgow & South Western Railway* how the rival Arran Boat Trains would race side by side along the sandhills at Ardeer with the drivers shaking their fists at one another! For its part the North British Steam Packet Company offered a more leisurely daily excursion from Craigendoran that called at Dunoon, Corrie, Brodick, Lamlash and Whiting Bay. Return fares from Glasgow to any destination in Arran in the late 1890s were 4/9d First Class and 3/6d Third Class. Throughout the 19th century Arran's holidaymakers were mainly of the upper classes. Most wealthy families who holidayed on the island took the let of a large villa for several weeks or months in summer and arrived complete with servants. By the 1870s there were several horse-drawn coaches connecting with the steamers and travelling to various villages. Nowadays most visitors come in their own motor cars and the ferry service from Ardrossan is normally operated by the roll-on/roll-off ferry *Caledonian Isles*.

Arran's first road suitable for a wheeled vehicle was constructed in 1810 from Gortonallister (just south of Lamlash) for five miles to Brodick, and seven years later Thomas Telford engineered the road known as The String across the island from Brodick to Blackwaterfoot. Around the same time the Duke of Hamilton had a road constructed from Brodick up the coast to Sannox. Other roads were built over the ensuing years, mainly in disjointed sections around the coast, and it wasn't until 1851 that the final sections were completed and the layout that we know today was in place. But more roads meant more traffic and as horse-drawn vehicles became heavier the roads had to be continually strengthened and widened. None of the island's roads were surfaced with tar until the 1920s.

Tourism on Arran reached its peak shortly before the First World War. It declined during the depression of the 1920s but revived in the 1930s. The years following the Second World War and into the 1950s were another boom period but it was followed by many lean years. The greatest change in the island's tourist trade in modern times came with the introduction in 1957 of the car ferry *Glen Sannox* which was the first purpose-built car ferry for the service. Since then, succeeding ferries have had steadily increasing vehicle capacities, resulting in an ever increasing influx of cars to the island. Brodick Pier and foreshore have changed out of all recognition since the 1980s, firstly for the introduction of *Isle of Arran* in 1984 and later for *Caledonian Isles* in 1993, both of them roll-on/roll-off type ferries.

Left: The Douglas Hotel on the seafront at Brodick was originally constructed in 1782 as accommodation for guests of the Duke of Hamilton of Brodick Castle and so it pre-dates the village. Later it was the local doctor's house and practice until 1852 when it became a hotel. The building pictured here, of locally quarried red sandstone and standing two and a half storeys high, was constructed in front of the original hotel building in 1858 and a dining room/function suite was added to the west side. Subsequent to the picture a large two storey bay has been added to the front north-facing façade and gives the hotel its present-day appearance.

A family group is standing outside the home of the Latona family in Brodick. Cosimo Latona arrived in Arran from Palermo in the 1890s, having married Blairgowrie-born Grace McEwan in Glasgow in 1894, and established this house as a boarding house which also provided boating trips for its clients and other visitors. In June 1893 *The Scotsman* newspaper gave an amusing account of the local Free Church minister having denounced Cosimo for the unforgivable offence of taking visitors for a row around the bay on a Sunday, and threatening him with being 'put down' and having the people rise up against him in rebellion. Cosimo, an Italian Roman Catholic, was unimpressed and forcefully told the minister to mind his own business. Typical advertisements for guests were inserted in the same newspaper in July 1906 and again in 1908 when the house was advertised to let 'for August or longer' and comprised two public rooms, six bedrooms, kitchen, scullery and servants' accommodation. In 1950 it was advertised for sale as having previously been a boarding house and comprising on the ground floor a large entrance hall, drawing room with bedroom off, dining room, kitchen, scullery and pantry. There were five bedrooms and a bathroom on the first floor.

The sandy beach at Brodick lies north of the ferry terminal and in this 1920s picture it is being enjoyed decorously by a number of families. No-one is actually bathing in the sea and all the holidaymakers are fully dressed so one can only assume that it's a chilly day. The beach huts were placed on the beach at the start of the summer season and removed after summer had passed but they are now long gone. There is no room for them nowadays because tides are higher and this has made the beach smaller.

This is the same location as the previous picture. In spite of the young men wearing kilts and one man wearing shorts, the coats worn by most of the remainder of the audience for this Punch and Judy show suggest that the weather still isn't at its best.

This photograph, looking north-westwards with the distinctive shape of Goatfell in the background, was taken from the shoreline just north of Brodick, probably in the 1930s, and shows the footbridge that carries the Fisherman's Walk (part of the Arran Way) over the Glencloy Water.

Cladach Sawmill, located adjacent to Brodick Castle, is on the site of an 18th century meal mill built to serve the castle. Nowadays it has expanded to include a garden centre and its products include sheds, fencing, timber, plants and garden supplies. Cladach itself is the site of the original village on Brodick Bay, the modern village of Brodick having been built later on the south side of the bay.

Goatfell (Gaelic *Gaoda Bheinn*) is the highest peak on Arran and at a height of 2,866 feet is classed as a 'Corbett'. It is claimed that on a clear day it is possible see from its pinnacle as far as the mountains of Snowdonia. It is a popular peak with climbers who have a choice of several routes of ascent, the most popular being an easy climb from Cladach or a shorter and steeper route from Corrie. These two climbers in 1907 have made the ascent wearing their everyday clothes – the one on the right is even wearing a starched collar and tie! The mountain is nowadays owned by the National Trust for Scotland.

These climbers in 1938 are doing it the hard way! They have chosen the harder route from Corrie and are scrambling up the pinnacles on the Stacach Ridge to join the others already standing at the top.

This row of sandstone cottages at Corrie Terrace, photographed in Edwardian times, was built for the quarry workers at the village's red sandstone quarry. Some of its output was used to build various public buildings on the island but most of its stone blocks were taken down to the southern of Corrie's two quays (known as the Sandstone Quay, as distinct from the northern quay which was known as Corrie Port) and loaded aboard 'puffers' for transportation to the mainland. The cottages were demolished In the late 1960s to make way for council houses and are remembered there by a street named Red Quarry Road.

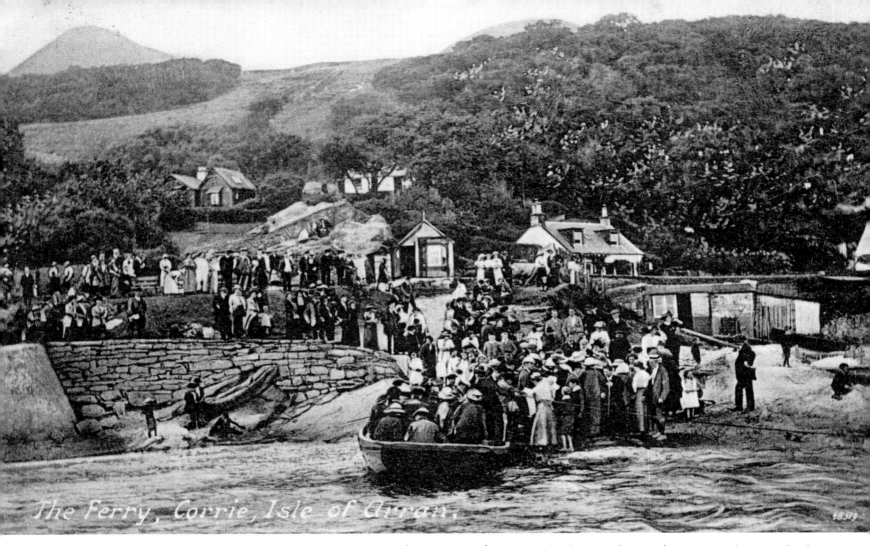

The Ferry, Corrie, Isle of Arran.

The village of Corrie, about six miles north of Brodick and approximately halfway to Lochranza, used to be a regular stop for steamers circumnavigating the island, with passengers being transferred to and from the ship by means of this rowing boat from the "ferry rock" which is located midway between the village's two quays.

The *Maggie*, registered tonnage 25 tons, was built at Ardrossan in 1877 and is seen here in 1885. The Mercantile Navy List for 1879 shows her as being a trading smack owned by Robert Logan (senior) of Corrie and twelve years later by his son. She had a long life with the Logan family because in the 1935 list Ronald Logan is shown as her owner. The following year she was sold to John Hill of Greenock and she also appears in the 1937 List but then disappears, presumably scrapped after 60 years' service.

Until the end of the 19th century Lochranza was one of the main herring fishing centres of the west coast with as many as 400 men making their living from it, and the bay was sometimes crammed with as many as 300 fishing boats. The boats were small, with a crew of four or five. The herring fishing brought prosperity to the village but the shoals of herrings eventually disappeared from the area and today the bay provides moorings for a relatively small number of pleasure craft. The tidal estuary of Loch Ranza forms a deep inlet in the north-west coast of Arran and the village is the most northern of the island's villages. After 1889 Clyde steamers called at the pier and would be met by horse-drawn carts and later by buses. This photograph, taken in 1922, looks out across the inner part of the estuary to the village of Lochranza on the other side. The four ladies are probably picnickers, the four boats tied up are fishing smacks registered at Ardrossan and the prominent building across the water is the Lochranza Youth Hostel.

This appears to be a family group with staff outside The Shieling which is situated at the far end of Lochranza, close to the pier from where there is a regular ferry service to Claonaig in Kintyre. Its ground floor flat is nowadays let to visitors throughout the year.

16

People, vehicles and animals are all waiting patiently for the ferry in this 1920s photograph of the landward part of Lochranza Pier, taken from the landing stage. The pier was built in 1889, went out of use in 1957 and was finally swept away in a storm in 1989. The summer service to Claonaig on the Kintyre Peninsula then had to use the small slipway until the pier was rebuilt in 2003, which allowed larger vessels easier access. Caledonian MacBrayne ships currently operate seven daily crossings to Claonaig during summer months and a daily crossing to Tarbert (Loch Fyne) during the winter.

"The queue for the ferry isn't moving so I might as well relax in comfort …. "

Cottages at Lennimore, Pirnmill.

The hamlet of Lennimore lies at the end of a short road leading inland from the coast road at Rubha Glas between Lochranza and Pirnmill on the west coast of the island. It appears that probably the whole population has tuned out for the photographer. Note the water butt collecting rainwater for domestic use from the roof of the cottage – it would be many years yet before the hamlet was connected to a mains water supply.

This charming photograph taken in 1922 is believed to be in the hamlet of Thundergay (locally pronounced *Thunderguy*) which lies just to the south of the previous picture. The man sitting outside his cottage appears to be trying to feed the donkey but the animal is living up to its stubborn reputation.

Pirnmill on the west coast of Arran is the closest village to mainland Kintyre across the Kilbrannan Sound. It is now flanked by satellite clachans including Lenimore and Thundergay to the north but at one time there were also an astonishing number of clachans and cottages scattered along the hillside. In the early days the villagers made their living from fishing, crofting, some illicit distilling and smuggling but in modern times they cater for visitors and tourists. Before the pier was built at Lochranza and bus services were introduced, steamers sailing around the island stopped at Pirnmill and visitors were ferried ashore by rowing boat. This picture shows a busy scene in the centre of the village in 1904 and one that is still recognisable today. Anderson's shop advertising sales of "provisions, groceries, refreshments, confectionery etc." has nowadays gained an upper storey with three dormer windows but its functions have hardly changed – it is now the village store and post office. The smithy next door has also gained a second storey and is now the Lighthouse Restaurant but is still called Anvil Cottage. Finally the house on the left has been increased in height but still displays its two dormer windows and porch in an almost unchanged appearance – this was a boarding house. The bridge in the foreground crosses the Allt Gobhlatch which provided the power for the mill in the next picture.

Mill House at Pirnmill housed the mill that made pirns (wooden bobbins) for Clark & Company of Paisley who later merged with their rivals J & P Coats. The mill was powered by a water wheel and was built to make use of the power of the fast-flowing Allt Gobhlatch as it made its way steeply from the mountains to the sea. It was built in 1780 but closed in 1840 when all the woodland within economic carrying distance became exhausted. By the time of this picture the mill and its house had been converted into one of the village's stores.

These intriguing cottages near Pirnmill were photographed in the 1920s. The two chimneys nearest the camera are standing on what was obviously once the gable end of a substantially-built stone cottage but which has been converted into these two wooden shacks. No trace remains today.

The Campbeltown & Glasgow Steam Packet Company included a ferry stop at Pirnmill in its itinerary, and for many years this was the only regular stop on the west coast of Arran. The village was served by small ferry boats that would row out to the steamers, and visitors would have to decant into them to be rowed ashore. The ferry call was maintained after the First World War but was discontinued during the Second World War and was never reinstated. In this 1922 picture passengers are landing from the screw steamer *Kinloch*. She was built by Messrs A & J Inglis of Glasgow at Pointhouse Yard and launched on 30th May 1878. In 1926 she was sold to the Channel Islands Steam Packet Company Ltd. and plied between Jersey and the mainland of France until 1929 when she was scrapped and broken up at Bo'ness.

A seaman at Pirnmill Ferry is shepherding passengers onto a rowing boat that already looks overloaded and would shortly be rowed out into the firth to board the Glasgow-Campbeltown steamer which would be either the *Kinloch* or the *Davaar*. This was often a hazardous enterprise and on 27th July 1923 the *Scotsman* newspaper reported that "About 8.30 yesterday morning the Pirnmill ferry boat, conveying some 50 or 60 persons who wished to join the steamer *Davaar* for Tarbert (Loch Fyne) was swamped a short distance from the shore and all the passengers were thrown into the water. There was some excitement but help was soon forthcoming and all the holidaymakers were got ashore not much the worse for their experience. Very rough weather was experienced in the early morning, and when the ferry boat was only a few yards from the shore a heavy sea completely swamped her".

A group of well-dressed people on the shoreline look to be waving their handkerchiefs in fond farewell to passengers on the boat as if they were emigrating to America rather than just sailing to Glasgow! The white-bearded gentleman appears to be so interested in looking at his pocket watch that he hasn't noticed in which direction the ship is heading!

The post office at Machrie, which at one time had been a farm, overlooks the Kilbrannan Sound with views across to Kintyre. The boards propped against the side of the buildings are advertisements for various items on sale in the shop, mainly cigarettes. The motor car is standing at the side of what is now the A841 main road and its pre-1931 registration plate shows it to have been registered in Liverpool. The first post office in Machrie was established in 1901 and was set up by Mrs. Weir who ran the whole operation from her own cottage. The post office was subsequently moved three times, finally to the building in the picture which was taken over by Mr. Sym who continued to run the business until 1954. Mr. Sym's customers could also buy groceries, tobacco and, if the occasion called for it, rent a car. The post office finally closed in October 1977 and the building is now a holiday let called Rowanbank Cottage.

Blackwaterfoot, at the foot of the Shiskine Valley, is the largest community on the west of the island and was originally just a small hamlet surrounding a harbour area which served as the main port for clachans in the valley. The land for the Shiskine Golf Club at Blackwaterfoot was originally part of Drumadoon Farm. The club was founded by Alexander Boyd, a banker based in Glasgow, and opened in June 1896. The course architect was the 1883 Open Champion Willie Fernie of Troon and he designed a nine-hole course. This was redesigned and extended in 1912 to eighteen holes by Willie Park (junior), winner of the Open Championship in 1887 and 1889. Six of the holes were on Drumadoon Hill and during the First World War they reverted to their natural state and fell out of use. They have never been reinstated, with the result that today's course is over the unusual number of twelve holes. No golf was played on Sundays until 1974. The larger building in the centre of the picture was the original club house.

23844 The Shelf, Shiskine Golf Course.

All twelve holes at Shiskine Golf Club have individual names and the formidable fourth hole, Par 3 and 122 yards long, is known for obvious reasons as the Shelf.

23849 Burncliff, Blackwaterfoot.

Burncliff farmhouse lies on the B880 road (The String) between Blackwaterfoot and Shiskine and was owned by several generations of the Robertson family. The byre is on the left, the new house with a date of A.D.1909 on the door lintel is in the centre and the original house is on the right. This photograph of Burncliff was taken around the time of the First World War but its appearance is unchanged today except for an additional window in the old house.

The name Shedog is a corruption of the Gaelic *Sheidog* which is literally translated as Windy Place. Until the 1930s it was Shedog hamlet that was the hub of industry in the Shiskine valley with several trades and public buildings, some of which can be seen in the background on this picture. Shedog now forms the northern part of the village of Shiskine.

Further down the island in a south-easterly direction is the hamlet of Sliddery which is in the farming heartland of Arran. This 1912 photograph shows the schoolhouse and post office, the latter being situated in the porch of the schoolhouse. The school was built in 1860 and drew pupils from Sliddery, Corriecravie and Bennecarrigan. It was described in the Buteshire OS Name Book as being "A very handsome schoolhouse with teacher's house attached, built by the late Duke of Hamilton. It is maintained by the Duke and the General Assembly of the Church of Scotland". At some time the post office was relocated to the village shop but following the closure of the school in 1946 both the shop and the post office were relocated to the empty schoolroom. The post office finally closed on 31st October 1981. The building is now a private house, but its appearance is unchanged apart from having modern single-pane windows.

Lagg is a hamlet on the southern coast of Arran, made up of a few houses and a hotel. At one time there were also two mills in the area, at Torrylinn and at Glenree. There was also a whisky distillery but competition from distilleries at Campbeltown and on Islay plus lack of proper infrastructure caused it to close in 1837. Happily this has now been rectified and a new distillery opened in Lagg in 2019. The family-run Lagg Hotel, seen here in 1910, is one of the oldest inns on the island. Dating back to 1791 it used to be a coaching inn with a few bedrooms on the first floor but the back of the hotel was extended in the 1950s and 1960s to create today's kitchen, large dining room and the majority of bedrooms. The well-dressed Edwardian people in this picture may have been staying at the hotel or they may recently have arrived on the waggonette which can just be seen, together with its horse, on the far side of the hotel. Bridge End cottage in the right foreground is nowadays Flaxmill Cottage, a self-catering holiday let.

Above: The post office was situated just beyond the hotel, at Kilmory on the other side of the bridge over the Torrylin Water in the wooden porch of James Cook's house and joinery business, where his wife Catherine was postmistress. It remained there from around the turn of the century until about 1920. The cottage in the foreground is Laggwood Cottage, nowadays a self-catering holiday let.

Left: An impressive array of washing has been hung out or laid on the bank of the burn to dry and bleach white.

Above: Two very serious-looking men resting on the boulders as the Torrylin Water gurgles behind them.

Right: It's a very pleasant walk along the path through Lagg Wood and along the Torrylin Water.

Lenamhor Cottages, Kilmory.

Lenamhor Farm is a short distance beyond Kilmory and down a minor road off the A841. The words on the picture say 'Lenamhor Cottages' and no doubt that was true at one time but they have obviously now been turned into farm outbuildings because chimney pots are missing, the thatched roofs have a forlorn and neglected appearance and unwanted items are piled up against the walls.

Kildonan, on the island's south-east coast, overlooks the tiny island of Pladda and has one of Arran's most beautiful beaches. The building in the centre of this picture is the former Free Church which was built in 1893 of sandstone with harled walls, a slated roof and a bell housing at the top of the eastern gable. Pictured here around 1912, it was the first church to be built at Kildonan and held 700 people but it closed in 1940 and was subsequently used as a bus depot. It is nowadays a farm building but is still identifiable as a former church despite its present dilapidated condition.

The village of Kildonan lies by the shore, away from the main road, and is named after the Irish monk Saint Donan who is believed to have lived here in the 6th century. A sub-post office was opened in 1934 to serve the more central parts of this strung-out village and was situated in the Kildonan Store (known locally as 'Cook's Store') at Auchenhew, near to the seashore. Its windows are festooned with advertisements for Rowntree's Cocoa and a solitary one for Cadbury's. Both the shop and the post office closed in 2009.

At one time Kildonan possessed the only coastguard station on the island but this was closed in 1981 and the Coastguard Officer for the island is now stationed in Lamlash. Kildonan Castle in the distance was built in the 13th century by the MacDonalds, Lords of the Isles and stands on the cliffs overlooking the island of Pladda and the entrance to the Firth of Clyde. It was built originally at least four storeys high in this position to defend against enemies attacking through the firth. The castle passed into royal ownership no later than 1406 and was granted by King Robert III to his illegitimate son John Stewart of Ardgowan. It was used primarily as a hunting lodge by the Kings of Scotland when the island belonged to the Crown but in 1544 it became the property of the Earl of Arran. In 1558 the castle was sacked and burned by the Earl of Sussex during one of the many raids made by English forces against the Scots. Because the Earl of Arran owned more substantial properties elsewhere he allowed Kildonan to slip into decay and it is nowadays a crumbling ruin, largely covered in ivy and, having become structurally unsafe, is not accessible to the public.

Pladda is an uninhabited island about half a mile off the south-east Arran coast opposite Kildonan and is privately owned. The lighthouse and its ancillary buildings were designed by Thomas Smith and are the second oldest in the Firth of Clyde. The light was first lit in October 1790. The tower was rebuilt between 1821 and 1830 and is seen here around 1912. The lighthouse tower is 95 feet in height and there are 128 steps to the top. Paraffin lighting with multiple wicks was introduced in 1870 and in 1876 the Pladda station was equipped with a foghorn (1 blast every 20 seconds).To allow mariners to distinguish it from the other lighthouses in the Firth of Clyde it also had to show a lower light from a small lantern 20 feet below the original one. This smaller tower was added around 1800 and created a double light which distinguished the lighthouse from the Little Cumbrae and Mull of Kintyre lights; it was discontinued in 1901 when the 'double lights' were replaced by a powerful flashing system. Under normal conditions its light (three white flashes every 30 seconds) is visible for 17 nautical miles. Provisions and other light stores used to be taken out to the lighthouse by boatmen but this changed in 1972 with the introduction of a helicopter service which was also used to transport the keepers to and from the lighthouse. The lightkeepers were withdrawn in 1990 when the lighthouse was automated and it is now remotely monitored from the Northern Lighthouse Board's headquarters in Edinburgh.

The establishment of a ferry service from Saltcoats on the Ayrshire mainland in 1790 transformed a group of tiny settlements in this area of Arran into the beginning of the Whiting Bay we see today. The bay faces east and from the 1830s onwards steamer services from Glasgow and other places on the Clyde Estuary that called at Whiting Bay attracted a very upmarket clientele for holidays. A golf club was established in 1895 and the village also possessed tennis courts, a bowling club and a putting green. The building of a new three-berth pier in 1901 allowed steamers to land passengers directly instead of by flit boats which were small rowing boats. As late as the mid-1950s the main ferry serving Arran from the mainland called at Whiting Bay as well as Brodick but in 1957 the change to a Brodick-only car ferry service led to a decline in the fortunes of Whiting Bay and the closure of the steamer pier which was subsequently demolished in 1964. A small jetty projecting out from the shore in the centre of the village is nowadays all that remains of what was once the longest pier in the Clyde Coast. The bay itself runs along the southern end of Arran's east coast and at low tide the beach stretches from Sandbraes in the north southwards along the entire length of the village. The A841 main road also runs alongside the beach and forms Whiting Bay's main street. In the absence of modern road vehicles from this picture, the scene by the putting green in Shore Road just to the south of the village centre is almost unchanged today. This photograph is 60 years old but even the style of the clothes hasn't changed much and the houses, hedges and garden walls all look the same today.

THE POST OFFICE AND SHORE ROAD, WHITING BAY.   97055.

This is the same location as the previous picture but the photograph was taken some 35 years earlier, around 1925, before the putting green was laid down. The building on the left contained the post office which was located in the downstairs room on the right, the entrance being round the side. It later moved to a small building in the centre of the village. The couple on the right of the picture appear to be holding a dog lead between them whilst their white dog enjoys its freedom over by the wall.

MAIN STREET, WHITING BAY, ISLE OF ARRAN   D 3939

Another photograph of the main street in Whiting Bay but looking in the opposite direction to the previous picture. This time the style of the holidaymakers' clothes and the models of the vehicles are a giveaway that the date is around 1960. The house on the right of the picture named Blairbeg was built in 1915 and was a popular tearoom and restaurant for many years but is nowadays the Wee Blairbeg Cottage holiday let. All the houses further down the road are still intact while the building on the left with its gable advertising the sale of fancy goods, tobaccos and confectionery is now the village post office.

This is a view from the pier in the late 1920s. The large building on the left is the village hall which was opened in 1926 and is nowadays screened from the road by bushes. Blairbeg House, still a private residence at this time, stands to the right of it in the picture. A cold day, judging from the amount of smoke blowing from the various chimneys, but that hasn't stopped a sailor from strolling on the beach with his girlfriend. The tearooms are long gone and have been replaced by the newer buildings of the Bay News and the Beach Hut. The gable of the building on the right nowadays belongs to M.B.S. Timber and Building Supplies which backs onto the scanty remains of the pier.

Another 1920s view from the pier, this one looking northwards and taken on the same cold day as the previous picture. The buildings along the seashore have subsequently fared badly because whilst the deserted small tearoom building featuring High Teas and Ices appears to have been since converted into a private bungalow, the remainder of the tearoom buildings no longer exist. Happily, the buildings standing on the other side of the road are still there today.

Moving further northwards along Whiting Bay, A. McKelvie's grocery shop which is close to the seashore is seen here in 1928. Today it is the Whiting Bay Stores, Newsagents and Licenced Grocers and stands at the far end of a line of smart-looking villas which are mainly hotels and B&Bs.

TENNIS COURTS, SAND BRAES, WHITING BAY.

213846. J.V.

TEA ROOM

The tennis courts at Sandbraes, pictured here in the early 1940s, are a long-gone feature at the north end of the bay. The nearest public tennis courts are now five miles up the road at Lamlash.

The island known as Holy Isle lies inside Lamlash Bay. It was originally called in Gaelic *Eilean Molaise* after an Irish monk named Molaise who spent some years living here in a cave in the middle of the 6th century. This name evolved into Elmolaise, then Lemolash and finally into Lamlash which was the name of the island until the early 1800s. After that time the name was generally attached to the village that grew up facing it on the main island of Arran and this small offshore island became known as Holy Isle. The island is a little less than two miles long and was bought in 1991 for £400,000 by the Samye Ling Tibetan Buddhists to provide a spiritual retreat for their monks and nuns. Day trips to the island for the public are provided from Lamlash between April and October but fires, alcohol and dogs are banned. There are two lighthouses on the island, the Inner Lighthouse and the Outer or Pillar Rock Lighthouse. This picture shows the Inner Lighthouse which stands on the south-west corner of the island opposite Kingscross Point on Arran and was built in 1877. It is 56 feet high and painted white with buff trim and a black lantern; its light flashes green for three seconds. It was engineered by David and Thomas Stevenson of the famous lighthouse-building family and is known locally as 'Wee Donald'. The lighthouse cottages were built behind it to house four families of lighthouse keepers but In its centenary year of 1977 the lighthouse was electrified and fully automated. This picture is dated September 1903 and shows an Edwardian party arriving on the island in a series of rowing boats, possibly gathering for a picnic on the rocks by the lighthouse.

A square-rigged sailing ship shows off her stately lines in the early years of the 20th century as she passes the Inner Lighthouse and heads down the Firth of Clyde.

THE PIER, LAMLASH

Lamlash, which lies three miles south of Brodick in a sheltered east coast bay facing Holy Isle, is the largest village on Arran in terms of population. It is also the seat of the island's local government offices and the location of the island's only police station, hospital and secondary school. In spite of this, its main industry is tourism and this is a wonderfully atmospheric picture of the bustling crowds of people at the steamer pier in the early years of the 20th century. The clock tower was built in 1885 and the notice board on its wall is advertising excursions to various parts of Scotland by the Glasgow & South Western Railway. Nowadays the pier has gone but fortunately the buildings remain, converted into holiday lets. During both World Wars Lamlash was an important and busy naval base and it was also a popular anchorage for the navy between the wars. Ships frequently took advantage of the shelter afforded by the bay which is sheltered by Holy Isle. Prior to the First World War visits from the North Atlantic and Home Fleets were great social occasions in the village.

BOWLING GREEN AND PIER, LAMLASH

545 / 131

Lamlash Pier was built in 1884, demolished in 1954 and replaced by a short concrete structure. During the Second World War the harbour was an assembly point for North Atlantic convoys and the village was the training place for No. 11 (Scottish) Commando during the early years of the war. Nowadays the bay is the yachting and leisure sailing capital of the island. The great pier may have gone since this mid-1920s picture but the bowling green still functions today.

The sandstone-built former Piermaster's house stands on the main road just north of the present pier and is nowadays a holiday let.

This early 1920s photograph shows the approach to Lamlash from the north with the grassed area on the left leading down to the foreshore. The ivy-clad building is Sillars Temperance Hotel which is now the Glenisle Hotel and, minus the ivy, looks almost exactly the same as in the picture. It was built in the late 1700s and was the home of Mr. and Mrs. Sillars until Mr. Sillars' death in 1858, at which point Mrs. Sillars turned the building into a boarding house named Sillars' Temperance Hotel. It remained the same after Mrs. Sillars' death in 1901 and was then run by her daughter until 1909. During both World Wars the building was used as navy billeting for commandos and after the Second World War it was sold and the name was changed to the Glenisle Hotel. The cottage on the right of the hotel was the local police station until a new one was opened in the 1930s. Set back from the road beyond the hotel, the picture shows the far end of the elegant terrace of houses called Hamilton Terrace, named after the 10th Duke of Hamilton who commissioned their construction. They was designed by Scottish architect John James Burnet and built in 1893 as two rows of idyllic single storey-and-attic white cottages for estate workers. Many are now self-catering holiday lets. The gable end near the centre of the picture belongs to Ship House but the row of single-storey cottages beyond it has been replaced by the modern Lamlash Bay Hotel. The church in the distance is Lamlash and Kilbride Parish Church, built in red sandstone in 1886 by architect Hugh Barclay in a Gothic style and with a tall campanile-shaped tower which houses a 9-bell carillon.

HMS Hannibal is seen here on a visit to Lamlash in August 1904. She was a twin screw battleship of the *Majestic* Class, launched at Pembroke Dock in 1896, commissioned in 1898 and sold for scrap in 1920. 421 feet in length and 75 feet across the beam with a displacement of 16,060 tons, she had two 3-cylinder vertical triple-expansion steam engines powered by eight coal-fired cylindrical boilers but in 1906 she was reboiled with oil-fired boilers. Her main armaments were four BL 12 inch Mark VIII guns in twin-gun turrets, one forward and one aft. Other armaments were twelve QF 6-inch/40 guns mounted amidships in two gun decks, 28 smaller guns and five 18-inch torpedo tubes. She was initially allocated to the Channel Fleet which was redesignated the Atlantic Fleet in 1905. By the time that war broke out in 1914 the *Majestic* Class were the oldest and least effective battleships in service in the Royal Navy. She had an undistinguished career and appears to have never fired a gun in anger.

Lamlash Golf Club is situated by the main road between Lamlash and Brodick and is the oldest golf course on the island. It is a hilly course of 18 holes, par 64, 4,510 yards in length and was designed by Willie Auchterlonie and Willie Fernie in 1889. Prior to the First World War during visits from the Atlantic and Home Fleets Naval personnel were welcomed at the golf club; in return they presented trophies that are still played for today. The Visitors' Book in the club's present-day more palatial clubhouse contains the signatures of the Prince of Wales (later King Edward VIII) and Prince Albert (later King George VI).

These 'Garden Houses' were located in the grounds of Altachorvie House which is situated to the east of the golf club and out in the countryside. In 1894 Thomas Arthur Leonard founded the Co-operative Holiday Association (CHA) and by 1913 he had established eighteen of these holiday centres around the British Isles. However, he then began to feel that the CHA had become too 'middle class' so he set up the Holiday Fellowship which had a simpler ethos and a greater emphasis on internationalism. In 1982 its name was changed to HF Holidays. These former Holiday Fellowship 'Garden Houses' are nowadays 'Sleep Huts' and are part of the Arran Lodge self-catering complex which includes the main lodge building of Altachorvie itself. Although quite basic accommodation, the individual huts nevertheless have en-suite facilities and flat screen televisions and offer budget accommodation for to up to 35 persons in 23 single, double and twin private rooms.